The Flying Whale

Written by:
Maria Habanikova

Illustrated by:
Marie-Pierre Castonguay

To Jack and Hannah, Hope you always have the courage to follow your big bold dreams!

Maria

Copyright © 2023 text by Maria Habanikova
Copyright © 2023 illustrations by Marie-Pierre Castonguay

Alll rights reserved. This book or parts thereof may not be reproduced in any form, stored in any retrieval system, or transmitted in any form by any means-electronic, mechanical photocopy, recording, or otherwise- without prior written permission of the publisher, except as provided by Canada copyright law.

ISBN: 978-1-7390375-0-5

Dedicated to:
Fiona, Jennifer, Lou, Natalie, Tamaira, and Tara

I am a flying whale.
I swim through the sky effortlessly.

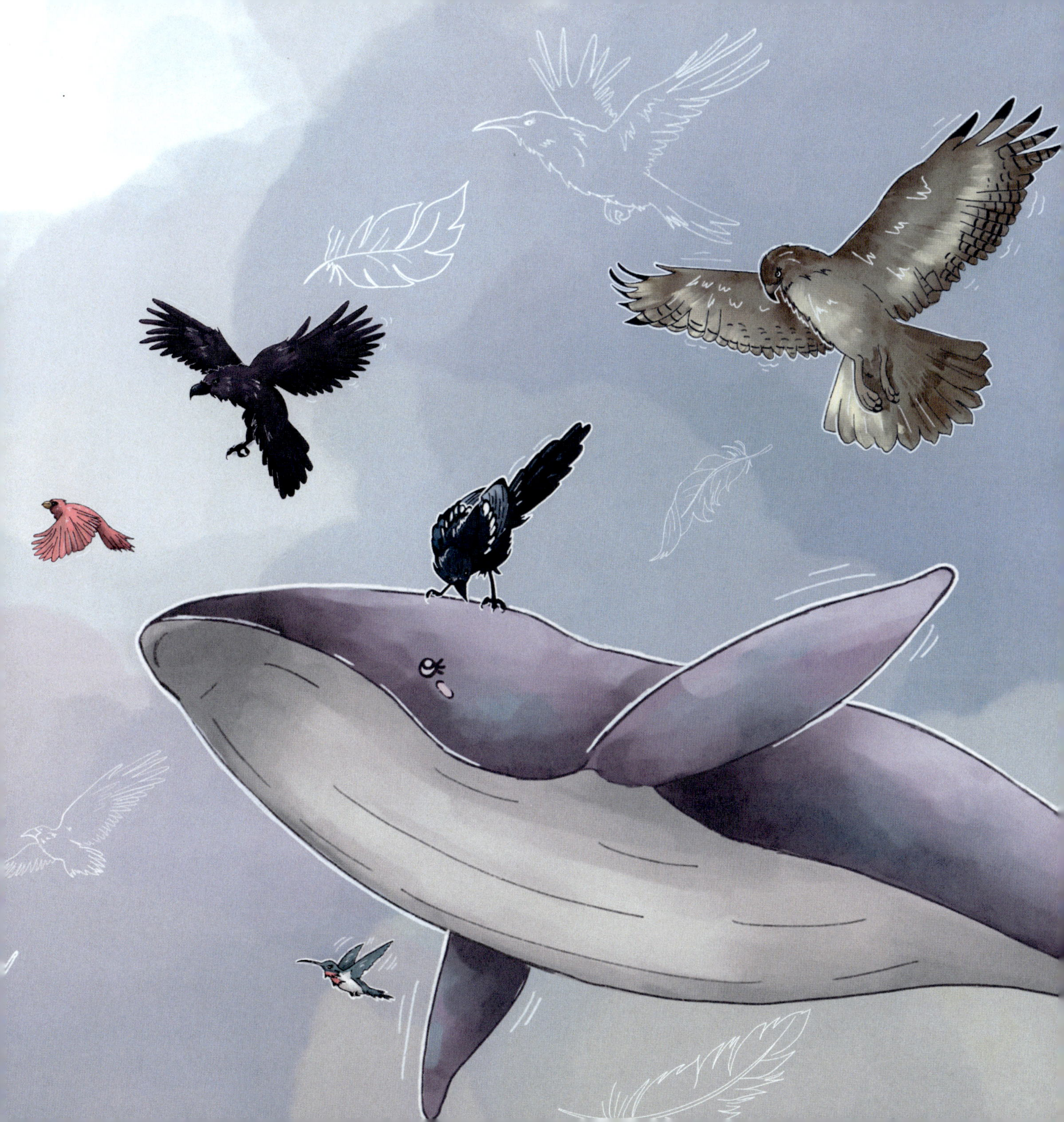

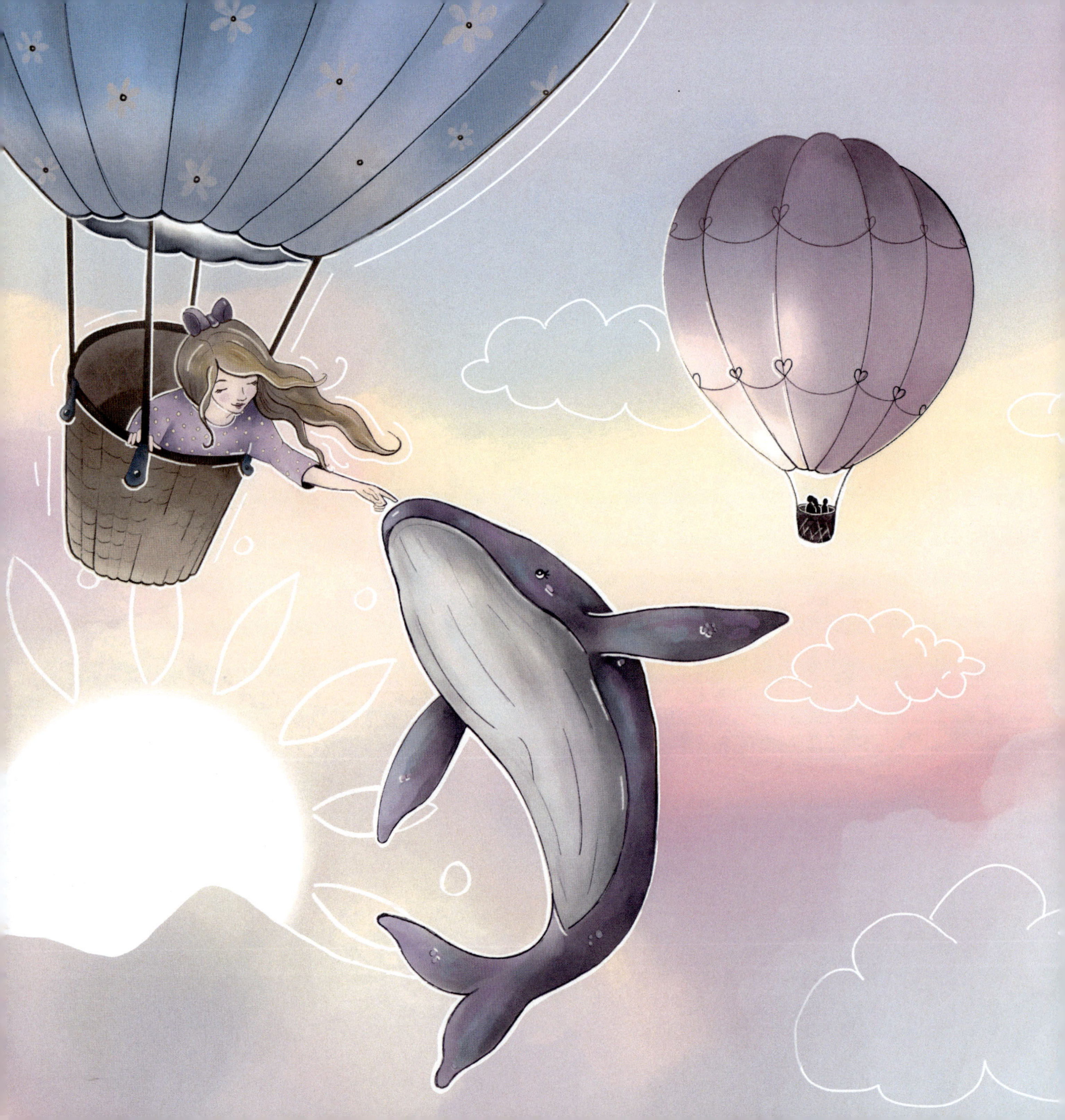

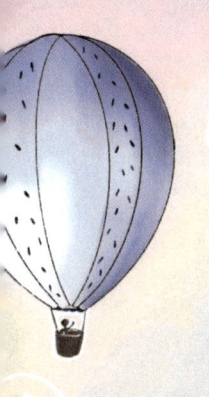

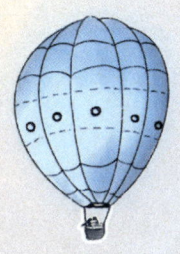

But whales don't fly, they weigh too much.
I am heavy with dreams lighter than air.

How did you get up there?

A rainbow carried me.

What do you eat?

Cloud cotton candy.

How do you sleep?

I rest among the stars.

How do you breathe?

With love.

It all seems impossible.

If you can imagine it, you can live it.

Let me show you.

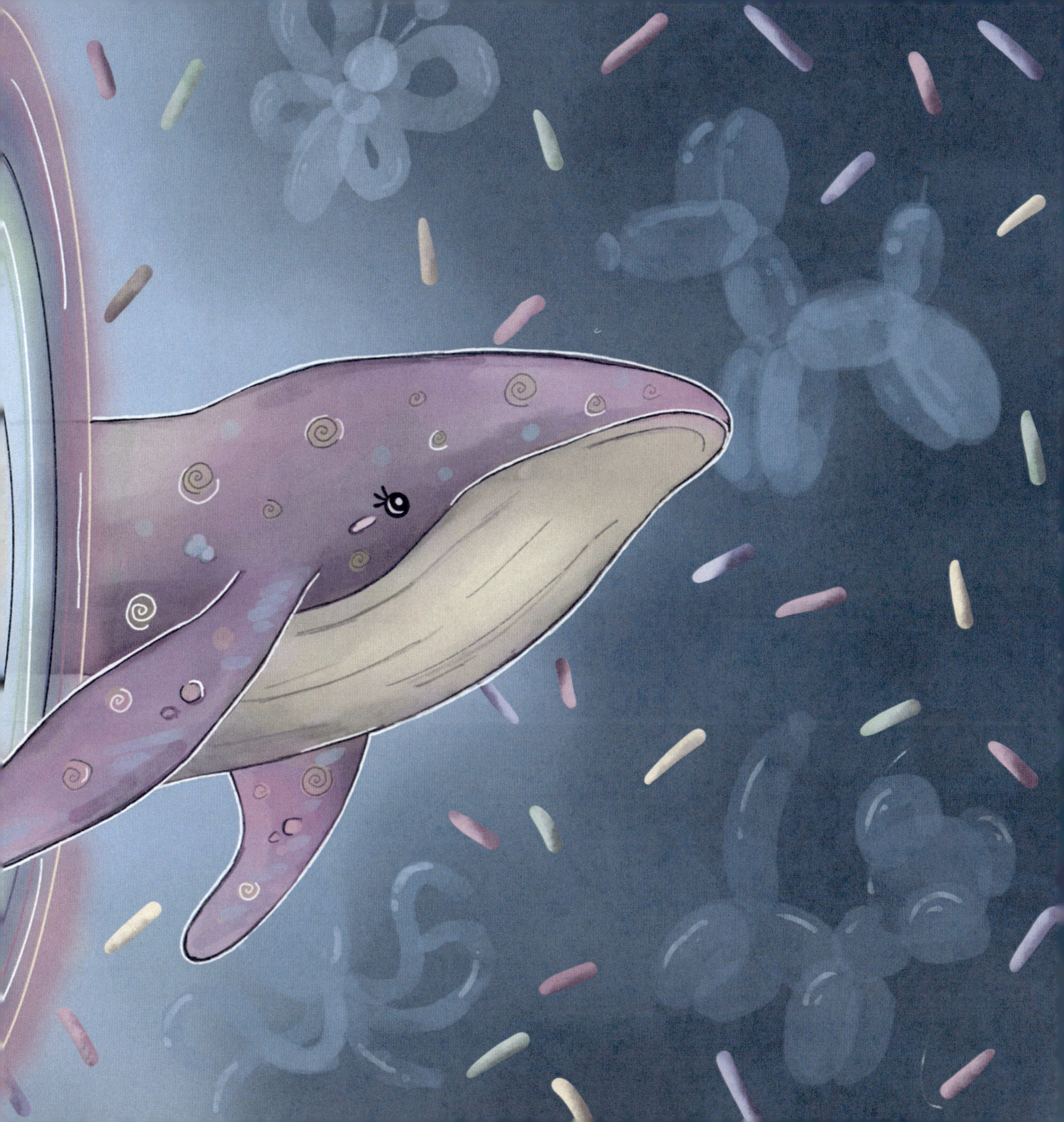

I am a bee,
I give life.

I am a hummingbird,
a tireless messenger of healing.

I am a doe,
gentle and patient.

I am a flying whale.

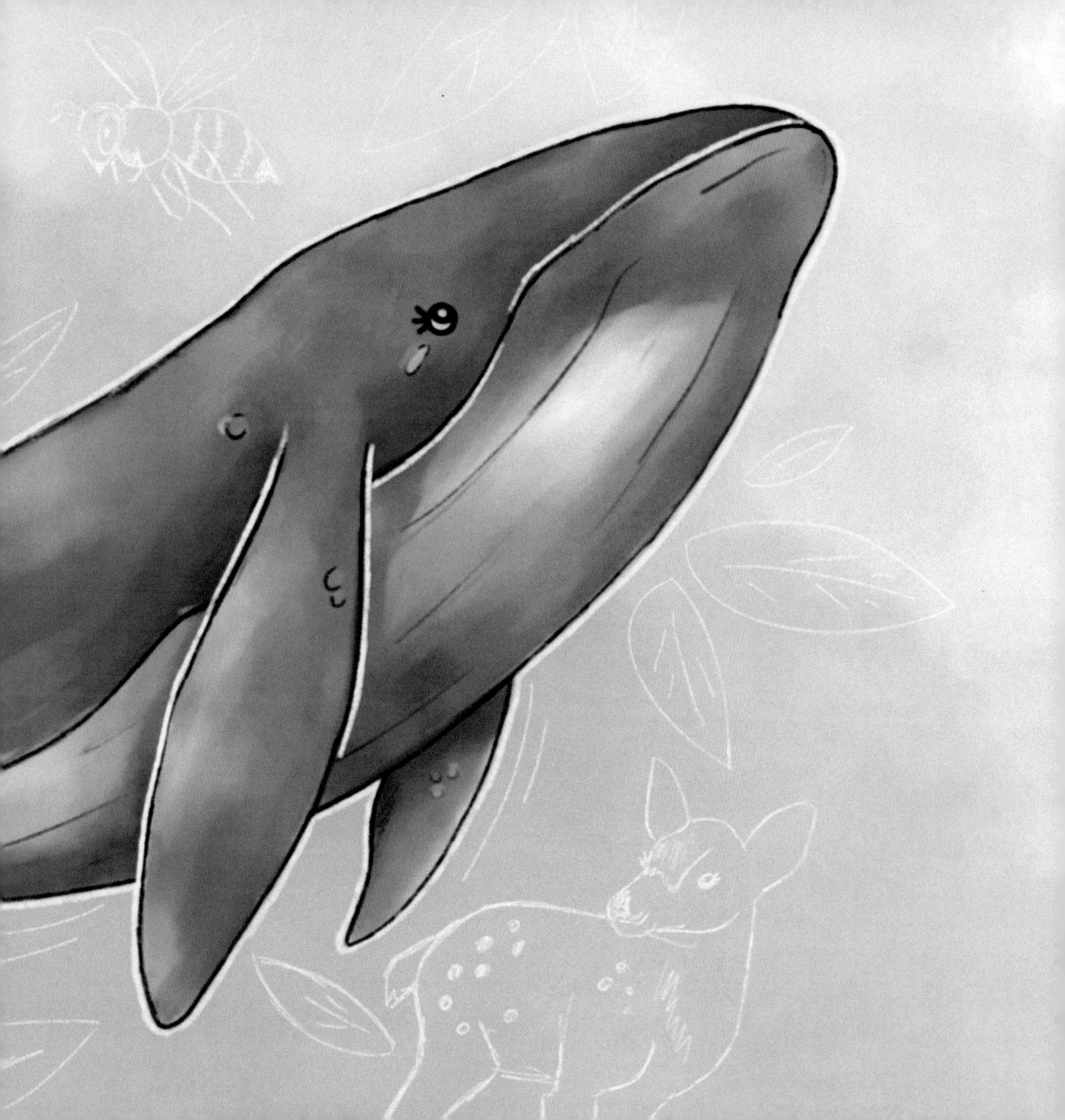

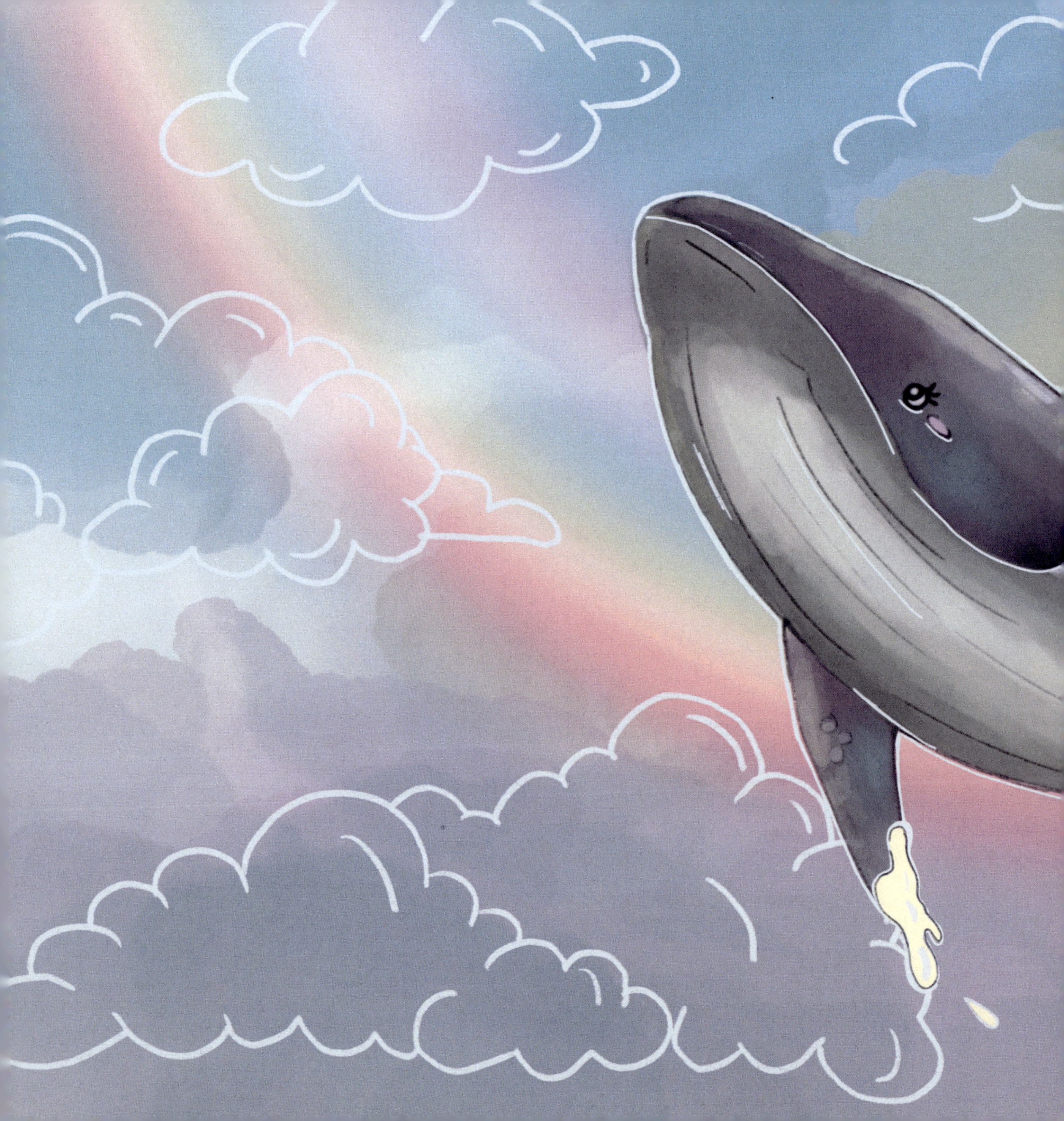

I painted the rainbow
and sweetened the clouds.

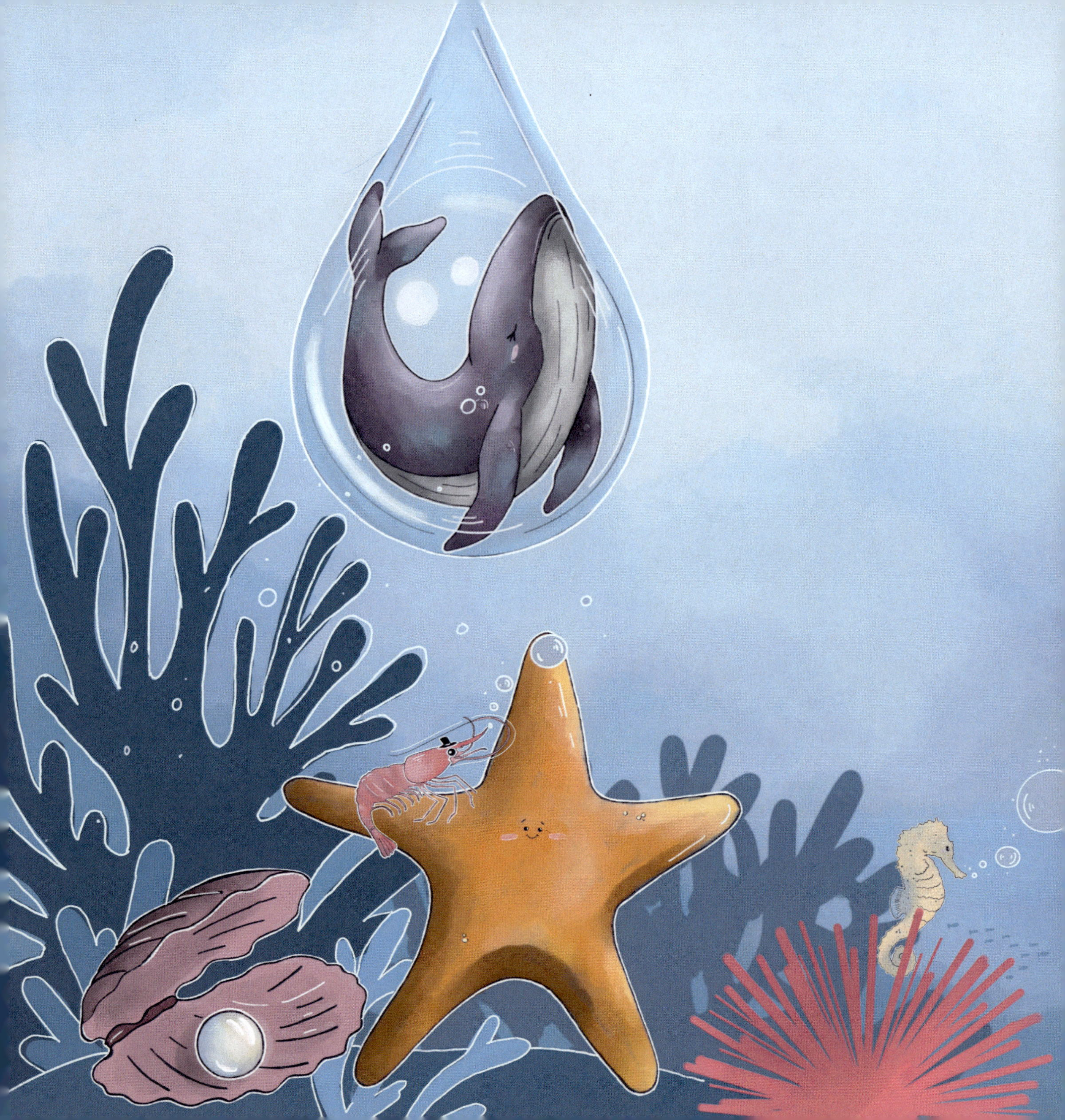

I am the **ocean** and a **drop** in it.

I am the universe.
I am a destination,
I am where dreams meet.

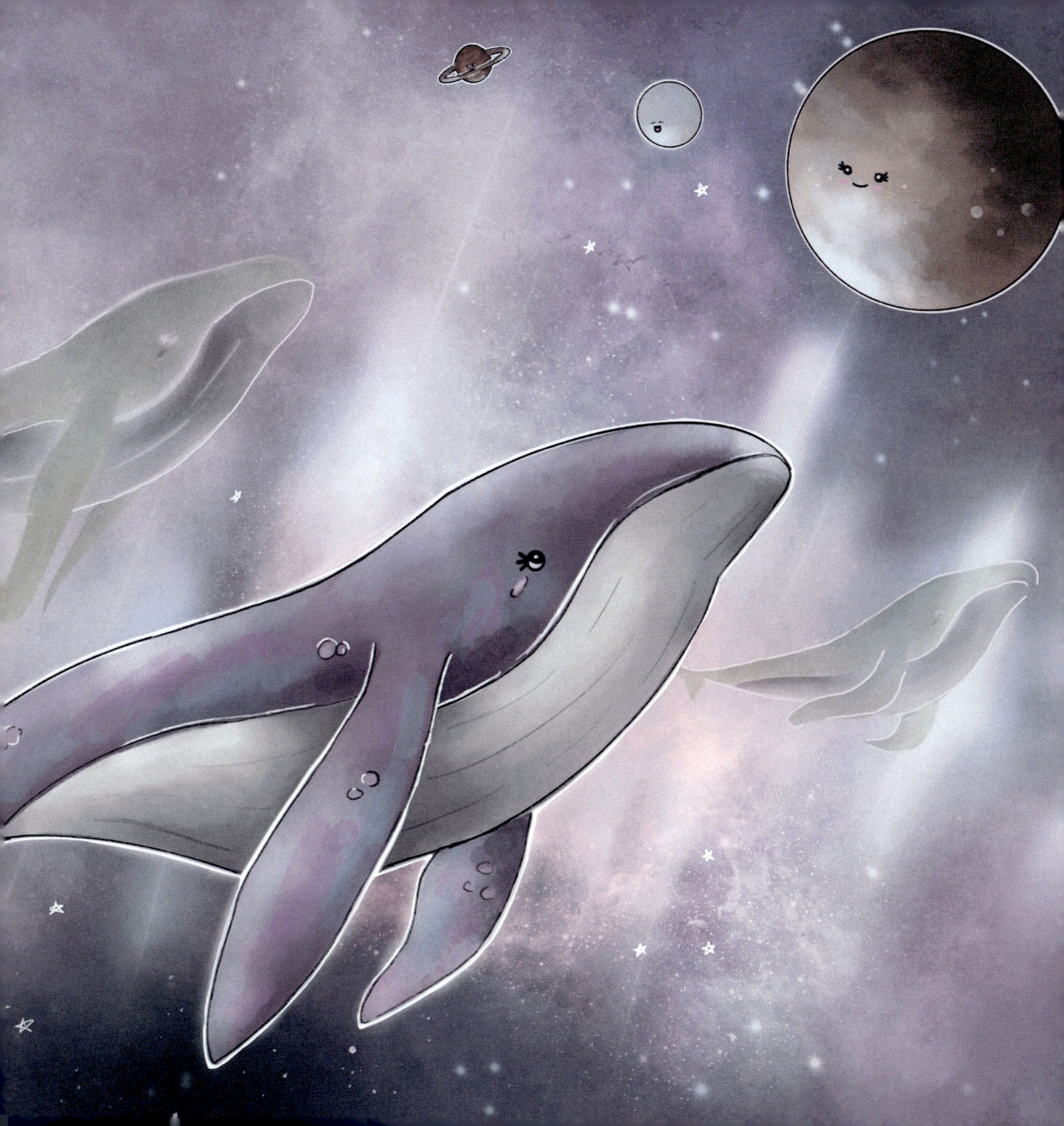

Whale Wonders?

1. What other questions do you have for the flying whale?

2. Can you name some of the species of birds that are swimming through the sky?

3. What does it mean to breathe with love?

4. How does a bee give life? Why are bees important?

5. Can you name the creatures under the sea?

6. Can you find a creature with a top hat in the book?

7. Where would you like to go if you could fly anywhere like the whale?

About the creators

Marie-Pierre & Maria

Maria is a true multi-passionate creative soul, a dedicated public servant at Global Affairs Canada, a Zumba instructor, and writing workshop facilitator at the Writers Collective of Canada. The inspiration for "The Flying Whale," her debut children's book, came to her on her flight from an ocean canoeing adventure off the coast of Vancouver Island with Outward Bound Canada in June 2018 as she was thinking about whales while looking at the clouds. Maria is a proud Slovak-Canadian and she lives in Ottawa.

Marie-Pierre Castonguay finds great joy and fulfillment in creating illustrations as a hobby. Marie-Pierre is grateful for the opportunity to embark on her second children's book project, following a collaboration with author Julie Armstrong on her first book, "Mushy Mushroom Couldn't Sleep." With each pencil stroke, she aspires to enchant readers of all ages, sharing her imaginative world and sparking a sense of wonder in their hearts.